Profitable New Bottled Water Business

Lee Lister is a Business Consultant with more than 25 year's consultancy experience for many household names. She is known as The Bid Manager or The Biz Guru.

From an early age she began an unparalleled journey through business consulting that continues to span across the UK, USA, Europe and Asia. She has consulted for many companies all over the world. Specialising in business change management, start up consultancy and trouble shooting. She is highly skilled in seminars, lectures and corporate presentations on business, project management and bid management. Lee's experience in marketing and internet marketing is also keenly sought after.

She is a prolific published writer of books, ebooks and articles on business, entrepreneurship and bid management. She can easily be found on major search engines and Amazon.

Profitable New Bottled Water Business

Learn how to set up a profitable business, understand how to overcome the strains and stresses of a new company and become a Successful Entrepreneur.

www.ProfitableNewBusiness.com

Author: Lee Lister

Profitable New Bottled Water Business

First published in Great Britain in 2009.

ISBN: 978-0-9563861-3-7

This book is dedicated to my daughter Kerry Lister for whom I have always strived to be my best.

Other books available include:

Entrepreneur's Apprentice

How Much Does It Cost To Start A Business?

Start My New Party Selling Business

Start My New T Shirt Printing Business

Start My New Cake Decorating Business

Profitable New Manicurist Business

Profitable New Quilting Business

Profitable New Bottled Water Business

Contents

Profitable New Bottled Water Business

Profitable New Bottled Water Business

Legal Notice

We do not believe in get rich quick schemes. We do believe that business is equal parts of inspiration, hard work and luck. We ensure that every book that we sell will be interesting and useful to our clients. Every effort has been made to accurately represent our product and it's potential. Any testimonials and examples used are not intended to represent the average purchaser and are not intended to guarantee that anyone will achieve the same or similar results

Please remember that each individual's success depends on his or her background, dedication, desire, and motivation. As with any business endeavour, there is an inherent risk of loss of capital. **There is no guarantee that you will earn any money**.

This book will provide you with a number of suggestions you can use to better guarantee your chances for success. **We do not and cannot guarantee any level of profits.**

This product is written with the warning that any and every business venture contains risks, and any number of alternatives. We do not suggest that any one way is the right way or that our suggestions are the only way. On the contrary, we advise that before investing any money in a business venture you seek counselling and help from a qualified accountant and/or attorney.

> **You read and use this book on the strict understanding that you alone are responsible for the success or failure of your business decisions relating to any information presented by our company Biz Guru Ltd.**

Introduction

Americans spent more money in 2007 on Bottled Water than on ipods or movie tickets: $15 Billion. An unlikely business boom or indulgence, whichever way you look at it, there is room for more businesses in the Bottled Water business. This is a business that you can start in a small way, but you need to be realistic in that Pepsi, Coca Cola and Nestle dominate this industry in a major way and your marketing budget is not going to bother them one iota. Nether the less, you will be able to make a comfortable living serving your local community or working in a similar niche. You just need to control your costs and build a memorable brand.

Getting Your Business Started

Many people are thinking of starting a new business and Bottled Water is certainly a popular choice. It is one of those businesses that you can run as a small business providing you are able to obtain the necessary business licensing and certificates. You should also note that in many countries the Bottled Water industry is heavily regulated and you may have to jump through a few hoops to meet these regulations before you can start out in business. Some countries will also insist that you are regularly inspected.

It is a business that you can run quite easily from home with just a telephone and a simple filing system as long as you are prepared to outsource the majority of manufacturing and distribution. Outsourcing the bottling and distribution of your water will usually assist you in meeting health regulations as the onus will be on the sourcing company to comply.

I have written this book with the presumption that you will outsource most of the bottling and labelling and so remain small. As you become larger and more established then you move to bottling and labelling in house.

You have the option of undertaking your own distribution or hiring a distribution company for yourself. It stands to reason that as you begin, you will be delivering your Bottled Water to hotels, restaurants, clubs and retail outlets yourself. As you become larger you will be able to afford a distributor to deliver the larger amounts involved.

You will also need to ensure that you have a working room that is both clean and well equipped to a professional standard.

It would also be good to have at least two checkable references. Once you have these you should take photocopies and put them in your sales pack.

Profitable New Bottled Water Business

If you have a good business plan, price your Bottled Water to make a profit are good at stock management and can build a good brand then this can be a lucrative business.

The Nasties

Tax, Insurance, Licences, Regulations and Certificates, these are the nasties of your business and all of them are compulsory! Look up your local state/county/country web site to see what licences and certificates you will need. Now look up your country's food agency website and see what regulations you need to adhere to. Similarly your country's tax web site will tell you what taxes you will need to pay, how you register to pay them and what forms you will need to fill in to become legal.

Don't attempt to work without them – there goes the way to a world of misery. Tax officials in particular, are trained to find and collect unpaid taxes and these are always combined with extra costs and penalties.

You may also need a sales tax permit (USA and other sales tax based countries) or VAT registration (UK and some Europe and Asia) if you reach the VAT registration limit.

Profitable New Bottled Water Business

Operating your business in some countries will require you and your staff to be licensed before you can start work. This should be displayed on your premises or available for view by your customers.

As you are handling food you will need to have various health certificates to show that you are trained in correct food handling, storage and selling procedures.

As stated before, some of the regulations can be adhered to by outsourcing the bottling and carriage of your water and this is the start up method that this book recommends.

What Is Involved In Bottling Water?

Well first you need a great source of pure water. So presuming you have this, how do you go about the rest of it? Well first of all Bottled Water is a very competitive area and one where products are bought because of their brand image so it is a difficult market to break into. This means that designing a great brand and testing your market is very important. You should also be prepared to spend a considerable amount on advertising and marketing.

1. **Water Collection:** I know it sounds silly, but you actually need a way of collecting the water and transporting it to your bottler. This could be as simple as a turn pipe or well and a truck, or as complex as a piping it direct to the bottling yard – depends on how much you want to invest. Start small is best.

2. **Purification:** Your water needs to be purified and all the nasties removed. Your country's regulations will state what and how. This can be done by your bottler or you can buy the appropriate distillers to do it yourself.

3. **Bottler:** First thing to do is to find a bottler – without a company to bottle your water you are not going anywhere! You should check that they will undertake small runs, because that is what you will be doing first of all. Negotiate a good price with an even better price once you make larger runs.

4. **Brand:** Now you need a really good memorable name for your water. As I said before, the name is everything. You will also need a good catchy strap line and a reason why people will want to buy your water rather than other people's offering. A good USP (Unique Selling Proposition) will also help.

5. **Label:** Now find a good designer, you can find them on sites such as guru and Elance or even your local university.

6. **Pricing:** In this competitive area, you need to get yourself a really keen wholesale price that will give your retailers a great profit.

7. **Marketing Strategy:** Now put all the above together and write a really great Marketing Strategy – that is how you are going to sell your products, at what price and to whom!

8. **Fulfilment:** Remember that you will need to get the bottles from the bottler to your warehouse or directly to the retail outlets at the beginning of your business. So you need to work out how you are going to do this and also how you are going to bill your retailers and collect the money.

9. **Testing the Market:** Now you need to do some testing to make sure that you really do have a viable product. Do a small run and get the Bottled Water into as many retail areas as you can within a small geographic area. This keeps your distribution costs down and allows you to easily check up on its progress.

10. **Results:** If all goes well, then sit down and update your business plan so that you can set up your new business. If it does not go so well then make any changes you need to – or decide that it was not a business opportunity anyway.

Good luck your new business is on its way.

What Kind Of Bottled Water?

There are many types of Bottled Water. You might want to be a generalist or you might want to specialise in one kind of Bottled Water. So what is the difference between the various kinds of bottled water, such as spring, mineral, purified, artesian, and others? The simple answer is purity. The determining facts of purity are:

- How the water is distilled or cleaned.
- The source of the water.

The FDA in the USA has established a Bottled Water Standard of Identity to define the several different types of bottled water based on specific characteristics of the product. Bottled water products meeting the Standard of Identity may be labelled as bottled water or drinking water, or one or more of the following terms:

Artesian Water/Artesian Well Water

Bottled water from a well that taps a confined aquifer (a water-bearing underground layer of rock or sand) in which the water level stands at some height above the top of the aquifer.

Mineral Water

Bottled Water containing not less than 250 parts per million total dissolved solids may be labelled as mineral water. Mineral water is distinguished from other types of bottled water by its constant level and relative proportions of mineral and trace elements at the point of emergence from the source. No minerals can be added to this product.

Purified Water

Water that has been produced by distillation, deionization, reverse osmosis or other suitable processes while meeting the definition of purified water in the United States.

Other suitable product names for bottled water treated by one of the above processes may include "distilled water" if it is produced by distillation, "deionised water" if it is produced by deionization or "reverse osmosis water" if the process used is reverse osmosis.

Sparkling Bottled Water

Water that after treatment, and possible replacement with carbon dioxide, contains the same amount of carbon dioxide that it had as it emerged from the source. Sparkling bottled waters may be labelled as "sparkling drinking water," "sparkling mineral water," "sparkling spring water," etc.

Spring Water

Bottled water derived from an underground formation from which water flows naturally to the surface of the earth. Spring water must be collected only at the spring or through a borehole tapping the underground formation feeding the spring.

Profitable New Bottled Water Business

Spring water collected with the use of an external force must be from the same underground stratum as the spring and must have all the physical properties before treatment, and be of the same composition and quality as the water that flows naturally to the surface of the earth.

Well Water

Bottled water from a hole bored, drilled or otherwise constructed in the ground, which taps the water aquifer.

You could also look at producing water to meet different markets and often in a crowded market it is important to look for niches here are some other examples of niches you can look at:

- High end for expensive restaurants.
- Small bottles to fit into packed lunches.
- Locally branded bottles.
- Sports Team or Club branded.
- General water for everyday very popular in recessionary times.

- Vacation branded – e.g. Halloween, Christmas etc.
- Occasion branded – e.g. the happy bride and groom, junior's birthday etc.
- Customer branded – e.g. Bill's Steak House.

Whichever type of water/s you decide to produce it will be important to build up a memorable and attractive brand image of each of your bottles. It therefore seems appropriate to start small.

Will I Succeed?

You've got a great idea, you are pretty sure that what you have will sell; you've even got some cash together. Have you got what it will take to succeed? What else do you need?

Vision: You must be able to see where you are going and what the future will hold. See what others are not able to see and build your business on these visions.

Courage: The ability to act upon your vision despite having doubts. The readiness to give up job security and a planned future; for the chance of making a success with your new business. This takes courage.

Strategy: Having the courage to act upon your vision, you now need to build your strategies. You will need a business and a marketing strategy.

These are the formulas that you will use to drive forward and manage your business.

Planning Skills: To ensure that you reach your vision, you need copious amounts of planning. Planning how you will reach your targets, how you will meet new changes and challenges and how you will improve your business. You will need a business plan and a marketing plan.

Researching: Having decided what your business is going to be, then you will need to find out who will want to buy from your business and at what price. This takes a fair amount of researching.

Conceptualising: Knowing what you want to sell and to whom, you now need to define your products and services. Brainstorm different things that you associate with your company. Include everything, good and bad, until you are out of ideas.

Keep in mind that ideas generate ideas. Write everything down, this is how you move your company forward.

Use this period to design your products, what you want your company to look like and how you want it to be perceived by your customers.

Creativity: You will need the ability to think outside of the box. Keep ahead of your competitors by coming up with new, unusual and unique concepts and solutions to their needs. You will need to create marketing materials, packaging and sales pitches – all will need verbal and visual creativity.

Determination: Along the way you will come across many hurdles and set backs, you will need to dig deep, make your changes and keep going. Determination and the belief in your visions and plans will keep you on the road to success.

Humour: When the entire world seems against you and all seems to be going wrong, when your customers seem to be your worst enemy then you need a sense of humour to carry you forward.

A Successful Business Start up

Right you have sorted out your business ideas, you are ready to go ahead and you know what you want to sell and to whom. Now you need your business structure. These are all the things that make up your business. They include:

- **Legal Base:** This includes such factors as your licenses, insurances and setting up your company.

- **Your Market:** You need to decide who you want to market your services to and where they will be.

- **Your Services:** You now need to decide what services you are going to offer to these people, how you would like to package them and what prices you wish to charge.

- **Your Business Plan:** Whether you are looking for funding or not – a business plan is the foundation of a new business.

- **Your Funding:** You should now take your business plan and look around for funding, starting with your Bank.

- **Your Premises:** Look around for your new premises, preferably in the middle of your potential market. Remember that central to your success is the position you choose for your business. Foot traffic past your door and many potential customers within a short journey from your new business is vital to you finding customers.

- **Web Site:** Most businesses have them now – so even if you don't want to set one up now – at least buy and hold onto your domain name – in case someone else gets hold of it.

- **Your Staff:** Good staff that reflect your business ideals are vital so spend some time spend some time finding the best staff you can.

- **Marketing:** So important and so difficult to get right. Start with a good marketing strategy and go from there.

- **Grand Opening:** Make sure you make a splash and attract as much curiosity as possible.

Your Business Framework

When starting a business of what ever kind, large or small, there is a always a require framework or scaffolding that you have to set up. Not only does this make your business much more effective, but it also saves you from a lot of embarrassing and costly problems. When you start up your business, remember to tick off the 10 items below and you will have a very sound start to your business. Here is your framework:

- **Business Name.** Choose an appropriate name that sums up what your business stands for. It has to be unique – try and ensure that a suitable domain name is also available as you will probably want a web site as well. The owner of an established web site might cause problems if you give your brick based business the same name – so be careful in your choice.

- **Your Business Entity.** Obtain professional advice as whether to the best way to set up your business as a limited company, partnership etc. Then register your company.

- **Patents and Trademarks.** If you have unique products then you need to ensure that you have registered your patents before your start trading. Similarly any product names, mottos, selling tags etc should be trademarked. Take professional advice on how to do this.

- **Licenses and Permits.** Ensure that you have all the licenses and permits that you are legally required to have.

- **Insurance.** You may think that you don't need this but you do and will. So take out property, business, vehicle liability, staff and disaster insurance. A good broker can advise you.

- **Taxes.** A necessary evil I am afraid. Register with your local tax collector. Set up a good accounting system and hire a good accountant.

- **Employment Laws.** Establish what you local employment laws are and ensure that you adhere to them. Set up employee guidelines and handbooks. Make sure you hire and fire legally.

- **Banking.** Visit your local banks and find the best business bank account and credit card for you business. Always keep your business and personal spending separate.

- **Business Plan.** This is your carefully written plan on how you want your company to operate, what you want to sell, where and to whom. It includes your business and marketing strategy as well as your financial standing and projections. This is the foundation of your business.

- **Liquid Cash.** Ensure that you have enough money to carry your through the first few months of your business as well as any foreseeable troublesome times ahead.

How Much Does It Cost To Start A Business?

You've got your business idea, think that you will be able to get a good loan and even have your business plan being written but…. The one big burning issue is – How much does it cost to start a business?

Well you first of all have to be realistic and understand that you are unlikely to make a profit within the first six months of business – so you should also budget for your first six months running costs. So here is your shopping list:

1) **Purchase of lease/franchise/premises**. This will include any Realtor fees, deposits and other legal expenses. Even manufacturers need some kind of premises. To start with you can use a home office, but you are going to need somewhere to hold all that stock and marketing materials that you will soon need.

2) **Cost of fit out and purchase of new equipment.** This will include any work that needs to be done on your premises as well as any equipment you have to buy in order to start and run your business. Often you can lease equipment in order to mitigate high start up costs. This also includes a car or van to deliver your stock to your distributors.

3) **Cost to pipe and deliver your water.** You Will need to pay to get your water from it's source, distil it and get it to your bottler.

4) **Initial costs for your outsourcers.** It could be that your bottler and labeller will require some kind of deposit or up front payment. If there is retooling required they will probably want you to contribute to these costs.

5) **Labelling costs.** You will need to pay to get your label designed. This is an important part of your brand so should not be scrimped on.

6) **Six months worth of advertising and marketing.** This will be particularly high at the start as you establish your business. Factor in some cold calling as well as a launch party or opening day. Marketing will include a lot of local advertising in order to attract good distributors.

7) **Legal, regulatory, licensing and banking costs.** Your business will need to be set up correctly, licensed and have a good bank account. Sadly all of these require money. You may also need a payment processing service to use credit cards.

8) **Staff costs for six months.** Staff will be the basis of providing good service to your new customers. Make sure that you have enough money put aside to find them, train them and keep them! Much of your staff costs will be on a commission basis but you will still require admin staff and one or two "on staff" distributors and maybe warehouse staff as well. They will all want to be paid, often before you get paid for your sales.

9) **Outsourcing costs for six months.** It may be some time before you start to get a return on your expenditure, so it is a good idea to budget for at least six month's outsourcing costs.

10) **Uniforms, office and marketing supplies, packaging etc.** You will need to establish your brand. This means that your staff will need uniforms or at the least business cards and name tags.

You will need brochures, adverts etc. If appropriate you will also need standardized packaging and documentation. Your office will also need office equipment and supplies. You should also budget for designing your logo, brochures and adverts if you cannot do this yourself.

11) **Stock and supplies** – to keep you going for six months. This will include your bottles of course which will be a large outlay. As will your labels. Don't forget the trays they will be stored on as well as the shrink wrap they will be wrapped in.

12) **Maintenance for six months** – your equipment will also need to keep going for six months.   This includes your cars, computers, printers, copiers etc. Budget for a lot of printing ink!

13) **Any loans** that you have will also have to be paid.   Again look at least at six months or until you break even and can pay the loan.

14) **Your salary for six months** – lastly you will need to pay your own bills and maintain your family during this time. You should expect that for a short while your standard of living will go down.

Add this up and add 10% for contingency and some good luck.

Bank Loans

B ank Managers - So Necessary for your Business But.... Meeting with your bank to ask for a loan for your business is always going to be a challenge even if you have a profitable business. Here's a few ideas for you.

It's important to remember that your loan manager is probably a kind human being who has to adhere to the bank's rules on lending. The basic ones are:

- That you can repay the loan.
- The loan is business based and for a reasonable reason.
- That your business is viable and bona fida business.

Go to the meeting armed with:

- Your business details such as licenses etc.
- An outline of your business and how you see it expanding in the next few years.
- If you are seeking a large amount of money or have a new business then you must have a business plan.

- How much money you require and when you need it.
- How you will spend it and on what items.
- How your business will benefit, expand or profit from the loan.
- What collateral you can offer the bank – don't offer this until asked.
- When and how you will repay the loan.

With respect to what you should not say – try not to hide anything – evasion is not a good reflection on your business acumen. If you are asked a difficult question then answer it as honestly as you can – but by putting a good spin on it then you should come out sounding positive.

Common Business Mistakes.

All entrepreneurs have to learn from their own mistakes as they build their business, but wouldn't it be great to have some one tell you what the common mistakes are and how to avoid them? You Want a Successful Business – So Don't Do This!

–   **Believing that you will start earning straight away.** All businesses take time to establish themselves – even internet based ones. People need to know where you are, what you sell and most importantly, that they can trust your company to deliver what it promises. Expect to spend at least 6 months working away at your business before you break even – sometimes longer.

–   **Believing that you can set up a business and it continually earns for you.** Even a very profitable business needs continual management to ensure that your profit does not erode. Your products and marketing need to continually change to meet the changing circumstances in the real world.

- **Believing that you can earn whilst you are aware from the office.** Even if you fully automate your business and hire really good staff, there is always an element of "while the cat is away". That is why there are so many "absent owner" sales.

- **Being a single product company.** As good as your product may be, markets and tastes will change and so must you. If your product is very good – other companies will quickly take action to seize your market share by bringing in similar products at cheaper prices.

- **Not offering upgrades and enhancements.** It is far easier and cheaper to sell to existing customers. You do this by offering upgrades and enhancements to their existing products. You should have a group of products at several increasing price points.

- **Relaxing after you success.** Businesses need continual effort, management and improvements. Although a product launch is hard work, you should start on your next product shortly afterwards. This will give you sustainable success and several income streams.

- **Believing that a business can be established with little capital.** Marketing, infrastructure purchases, stock, advertising and staff all cost money and must be purchased in order to make a profit. Cash flow kills more business than anything else.

- **Believing that you know all you have to.** Your competitors may have been in the business longer than you have, your customers may be very knowledgeable. Meeting customer needs is a constantly changing landscape and you need to keep up to date on the latest trends and technology. You need to be able to project yourself as an expert in the field you work in. If you do not have this knowledge then learn it or buy it in!

- **Not investing in your staff.** Your staff are the public face of your business. They should be well trained, knowledgeable and well dressed as well as fully motivated to sell on your behalf.

- **Not motivating** your staff. Good staff are hard to find and difficult to keep. Good staff help your business expand and be profitable. Good staff will grow your business exponentially as word of mouth spreads so you must look after them or you may find them working directly for your client.

- **Not motivating** your distributors or sales staff sufficiently. Selling on commission only is very hard work, it must be rewarding and your staff should feel that they will benefit from it. Your distributors, particularly at the beginning will be chasing around looking for retail outlets, doing a lot of mileage, delivering stock and looking after retailers. So they need motivating and reward well. Good distributors will grow your business exponentially so you must look after them.

- **Distribution problems.** Once you get established, the geographic area you are selling to becomes larger. Care must be taken that you can get your goods to your new customers. The cost of mailing and delivering your items must be properly calculated and included in the sales price.

- **Stock Holdings.** With distribution problems comes stock holding problems, the more products you have, the more stock you must have. If you have different bottle sizes and colours this figure goes up even more! It is very important that you work out how much stock you need as stock is dead money hold no more and no less!

- **Branding.** It is important that your company is recognised and has a good image. This helps spread the word about your services! Otherwise why would your customers use you? Spend on your brand, it's worth it!

- **Believing in Get Rich Quick Schemes:** A good business is established by part inspiration, part perspiration and just a little bit of luck!

Learn these lessons well, avoid the mistakes at all costs you should save valuable time and resources by doing things right the first time. Good luck.

Your Start Up Needs

There are a few things that you will need on your start up. These will make you look professional and help you market your business.

Your Brochure

Your brochure can be quickly made up on a PC. Design a one page description of your business, your Bottled Water and why it's the best in it's field. Include your contact details and company name. Do not include too many words – just make it catchy, memorable and informative. You can include a couple of graphics which you can easily find on the internet.

Your Sales Pack

This is what you use when searching for new business or when newspapers, search you out. It is what makes your business professional. The Sales Pack must contain a printout or photocopy of your terms and conditions, insurance and background check, references and your brochure.

If possible you should also include some sample bottles or at the very least your labels and some graphics of your bottles.

If you wish you can also include a business card. These can be professionally produced from web sites such as vistaprint or from you local stationary store or printer.

In your terms and conditions you should explain the details of your working policy. This will give information such as: your hours of operation; when a deposit and full payment is due; if you will deliver or not etc.

In this way you look organised and professional but also avoid misunderstandings in the future.

Your Uniform

It would also be a good idea to give yourself some kind of uniform. You can buy smart aprons from large department stores or uniform stores or you can get t shirts or sweaters printed with your company name. Visit CafePress for some ideas.

Match your colours of your uniform and your equipment to your company colours. This makes you look like a professional company.

Make sure that everything is cleaned regularly – including your equipment so that you are always ready to work and look professional to your customers.

Equipment

As well as your uniform you might need a trolley to carry that heavy water as well as heavy gloves and a back support.

In your office you will require a good computer with accounts software as well as a customer relationship management database (CRM). This will allow you to mange both your accounts and your customers, sales and invoices.

Your Vehicles

You car will do at the beginning of your business but you should upgrade to a van as quickly as possible, this not only looks more professional but is easier on your insurance as well as your suspension – water is heavy!

Your van should be sign written. At the cheapest you can get vinyl stick-ons but painted is best. This is your travelling advert.

Bottling It

When you first discover that you have a source of pure water, it seems so easy to want to start a Water Bottling business – but it is harder to get your water into a bottle and then sell it as you probably first thought. So what is involved?

Boring

First of all you have to get the water from the stream, river, pool or well. The usual method is some kind of water bore. Boring will require a skilled engineer to undertake and is far too complex for an unskilled worker to undertake. More details can be found – courtesy of the Australian Government at: http://www.publications.health.sa.gov.au/cgi/viewcontent.cgi?article=1038&context=envh

I cannot emphasise too much that you MUST get professional advice and assistance.

Purity

Now you have to get your water pure and this is done using a distiller or a filtration system. This process will be heavily controlled by your country's food or health regulations should be taken as your guidance. You will find the appropriate machines necessary for this activity for sale via the internet. You may find that your bottle will undertake this activity for you.

What Bottlers do

Now we come to fun bit – bottling your water. There are actually machines that will undertake the following all at once:

- Hold the bottle.
- Fill the bottle.
- Cap the bottle.
- Label the bottle.
- Pack the bottles into trays of one dozen.
- Shrink wrap the case.

Bottles and Labels

As mentioned several times before, you must concentrate on the design of your bottle and label. If you doubt this importance then take a walk down the bottled water aisle of your local supermarket! How are you going to differentiate yourself from the hundreds of others?

Well bottle design is one option but that is an expensive option when your first start, not only in purchasing but also in bottling if it is an unusual shape or size. You are best to aim at a regular size and shape and perhaps look at a different colour.

This makes the name of your water – which we will investigate more in a later chapter – and the label very important.

Spend as much as you can afford on the label design and choose an eye catching, memorable one!

Pricing Your Product

Pricing is so important to the success of your business. When pricing your Bottled Water look at the following:

- Cost of the materials.
- Manufacturing costs to produce the Bottled Water.
- Packaging costs.
- A percentage of your equipment costs.
- Cost of your time.
- Delivery costs.

You should set some money aside to build up your brand image by advertising and training your staff. People are more likely to come to you if they know your product.

Now have a look at what other Bottled Water sellers are charging and try and ensure your prices are similar and that you fit into the correct niche.

Minimising Your Costs

In order to minimise your costs you need to:

- Ensure that you keep your stock to a minimum. Stock is money that you need to earn.

- Decide upon the optimum bottling levels. Short runs are more expensive than longer runs.

- Look at the most outstanding bottle and label design you can afford but don't use at non conforming bottle sizes and shapes if they are not cost effective.

- Manage your outgoings and ensure that all costs will result in an income – this includes adverts and marketing.

- Adhere to legal, hygiene and food regulations!

Branding, Packaging And Other Stuff

B randing is so important. It is how people recognise your company and what you are selling. People will more readily hold parties for companies that they recognise and buy products that understand and know.

Your brand is so much more than your logo; it is your company name, your web site and the colours that you use. Everything that your customers and staff see should be "stamped" with your company brand and be instantly recognised as belonging to your company. So let us look at where your will be using your brand.

The Name of the Water

The name you give your water is so important, it should be first thing that you think of. You need a short, catchy name that people will recognise as water.

You also need to trademark this name. Check that it has not been used for other things, is suitable. Spend some time and money with testing the name out with groups of people and see what they think of it. You should also try and get the domain name as well. This protects you on the internet.

Label

As mentioned before, this is important. The label should reflect your water's name and the brand that you are trying to reflect. It is no good trying to be "cool and refreshing" if you use and antique design.

Packaging

It stands to reason that all your packaging, including that used in delivering your items, should be stamped with your company name, logo, phone number and web site. All packaging should include further Order Forms when you start off.

Invoices and Order Forms

They should have your company details, contact details and web site as well as your logo.

Marketing Material

Once again you should market such that your company and how to contact it, is instantly recognisable. How and where you advertise should also back up your brand image. If you are selling family friendly items then you would not advertise in a "lad's mag" for example.

Website, store, kart, market stall

However you sell your goods, they must have your logo and contact details emblazoned over them as well as completely reflecting your brand.

Some Branding Ideas

Your Bottled Water name, label and brand can reflect lots of ideas. Here are a few to get your brain ticking over.

- Cool and refreshing.
- High end, for the top people only.
- Quick and easy to use.
- Good for the kids.
- Restaurant use.
- For lunch boxes or picnics.
- Best for barbeques.

You can also look at providing bottles with labels for:

- Clubs.
- Sports fan.
- Weddings.
- New baby.
- Baby showers.
- Wedding celebrations – e.g. Golden.
- Parties.

Your Premises

This is a retail business that is not suitable to run from your home base, except in the very beginning. You could work from your home garage or a local warehouse, but you really need a retail outlet to advertise your Bottled Water. Why not think about starting a kart or kiosk in a shopping mall or a stall in a local market? Here are a few points to consider.

Mall Karts and Kiosks

As always Location, Location, Location: The location of your business is crucial to its survival. A store's location can often spell its success or failure. Without sufficient store recognition, a business can suffer poor cash flow and will inevitably fail over time. Your business needs to be physically located out in midst of everyday life, in broad daylight where shoppers can easily find you.

The location itself of the mall plays a huge role in your kart's success. Is the mall located in an isolated part of the city or town, or right in the heart of the action? You must forecast the level as well as the timing of traffic your business will receive during the morning, midday, and late afternoon on each day of the week. Therefore, you can efficiently establish an employment schedule as well as appropriate operating hours.

Choose your mall carefully so that it has ample traffic of potential customers. Go there with a "clicker" and see how many people pass by per hour. Visit on several different days of the week as well as at different times.

Quality of Traffic: It is one thing to have steady traffic, and another to have the kind of traffic that your business needs. Some malls attract low-to-middle income people; others are targeted towards the upper class. Choose wisely.

Profitable New Bottled Water Business

Position in the Mall: Your success in a mall will depend on whether you are located in a section that is conducive to what your business is selling. You should look at the **complementary nature of the adjacent stores.** If you are a gourmet store, you may want to be located near a restaurant where people are already in their "hunger fulfilling" state of mind. Complementary businesses, such as fine jewellery and gourmet food, have also been proven to work well together as both its customers are likely to have disposable income and a tendency to spend for these two genres of luxury products.

Similarly **high volume areas** where lines of patrons form, such as theatres or department stores, are also good mall locations as it could give potential customers several minutes to look in your display or listen to your sales pitch.

Costs: Rental costs in shopping malls are often higher than rates in downtown Main Street. You main consideration should be: will the higher traffic compensate for the increased rental cost?

If you can easily recover your monthly rental payment and overhead expenses, you're in a good position to make a profit.

People Buy with their Eyes! Lastly ensure that you display your products in an tempting manner. Karts and Kiosks are very good in selling items that are "impulse buys". Make your products appealing and your sales pitch interesting and your sales will increase!

Lastly, as business improves, you can easily buy or lease another kart!

Market Stalls and Boot Fairs

The same criteria about location appertains to market stalls and boot fairs. Obviously your outlay will be much smaller – but so will your potential income. Care should be taken to ensure that your stall looks professional and well branded otherwise your business will be classed as a "hobby business" and people will expect to pay correspondingly low prices.

Warehouse

Obviously hundreds of cases of Bottled Water need to be stored somewhere. The cheaper option is to store with your bottler. This saves one set of transport. This may not be possible of cost effective or you may just want your own warehouse. In this case you will need to look for a suitable sized warehouse. You will also need a forklift to load and unload as well as your van to transport your bottles.

Marketing Your Business

N ow we need to market your business. You will need to find both retail buyers as well as distributors. You should be aiming your marketing at the following:

- Retail outlets such as local stores, delicatessens, small local supermarket chains etc.
- Hotels, restaurants, pubs and cafes.
- Clubs and sports arenas.
- Wedding and party planners.

Whilst it is tempting to aim for the large supermarkets and chains, you need to get yourself established first. It will be more fruitful to aim as small, local chains who will be more receptive.

Onsite Marketing

Whichever low cost option you chose, ensure that you have plenty of brochures available to give out to interested potential customers. Don't leave them on the counter otherwise you will go through a lot of them for little return – save them for the really interested people.

You could leave business cards for anyone to take- people tend to take these only if they are interested.   You should display some good samples as well as a lot of items for sale.   Be prepared to take orders from your stall.

Local Adverts

Set up an advert on your PC. You can print them off, on postcards quite easily.   It should read something like this.

Bottled Water
Bottled Waters for births, celebrations and weddings (*or whatever your brand is*)
Call CompanyX: 123-4567
ABC Bottled Waters

Alternatively you can visit Vistaprint or your local printer and purchase some very colourful postcards. You now have a professional advertising "billboard" that will be eye catching and hopefully memorable. People tend to keep postcards longer than paper adverts or business cards. They are also unusual enough to attract attention.

Now is the time to use a bit of shoe leather. Put the cards on notice boards in supermarkets, shops, clubs, offices etc. Always ask first. You can also put a similar advert in your local papers if that is affordable.

If you also decided to use business cards – use the front to put your company name, contact details and a one line description of your services and on the back put your short advert. Leave these wherever you are allowed to and concentrate on where you will find your potential clients.

It takes a while to start up any kind of company. Start touting for small contracts to begin with particularly those that you can do yourself. As you get more work or get offered larger contracts you can start to consider taking on staff.

Sales Packs

Set up an sales pack. It should be quite small – say A4 or A5 and a few pages. It will include details of your company and products as well as a few samples, your prices and some great photos of Bottled Water. Include some references if you have them. People like to know that you have some good customers already.

This will be given to prospective customers who are seeking to purchase your Bottled Water.

Shoe Leather

You've got everything together and have got a warehouse full of bottles, so what do you do next? Well you find large retailers or distributors that will look for customers on your behalf. Here's a way to go about it:

- **Research:** Use the internet, yellow pages, library, local magazines etc.

- **Plan:** List your potential customers and decide how many you will visit a month.

- **List:** Set up a weekly list.

- **Contact:** Contact the relevant person by phone if possible. Send them your sales pack and a sample of water. Ask for a meeting to discuss matters. Use a script if it helps.

- **Confirm**: The receipt of the sales pack and ask for a meeting if you don't have one already.

- **Meet:** Take samples, go into your sales talk and ask for an order.

Finding Retail Sales

Look for opportunities to pitch to clubs, sports groups, local arenas, wedding and party planners. If you get the opportunity of a meeting then take your sales pack with you and listen to what they require. Be prepared to provide small runs of your Bottled Water with bespoke labels on them. Ensure that you know your prices before the meeting and be ready to quote for 100, 250, 500 bottles etc.

Have a look at our contract chapter to ensure you understand how to seal the deal legally.

Finding Distributors

Distributors will enable you to shift a lot more Bottled Water at a time. Establish your brand by selling to a few retailers so that you have a track record and some references. When chasing distributors, ensure that you have enough Bottled Water in stock to meet their needs. You will hopefully be moving more Bottled Water in the future.

Pitching to Win and Winning that Pitch

You've got a viable product, you know that this large company would be very interested in it – you are now entering a high risk area – pitching your product to a much larger company.

A couple of things to think about before you start. The large company has more resources, more money and more lawyers at their disposal so you need to protect yourself as much as possible first of all.

Secondly, are you sure that your idea is not one that the large company is presently developing? They won't tell you of course, but if your product is an enhancement of one of the large company's existing products, then don't be surprised if you are turned down and "your" idea comes to the market shortly afterwards.

Now you need to prepare:

- Make sure you have a trademark for your Bottle Water name. This is so important and provides you some protection if your concept is stolen.

- Investigate your target company and fully understand what they sell and to whom.

- Understand how your product will fit into their product range.

- Define what benefits the target company will obtain from your new product.

- Produce an overview of likely costs and benefits to your target company. Companies will only be interested in a new product that makes them a healthy product.

- Take samples of your product, with packaging, if you have got this, as well.

- Prepare a good presentation – lasting about 10 minutes that will hopefully spark interest in your new product.

- Have a good understanding of what you hope to achieve from the pitch – sale of the distribution, licensing or partnership.

Lastly, be confident, clear AND listen to what the large company are saying – they have been in the business for longer and are more successful than you are – they must be doing something right.

So if you plan to present your Bottled Water to a large company, be prepared to do so completely at your own risk. Look up the story of Dyson to learn some valuable lessons.

Your Sales Meeting

Once you spread the word that you're in the business of Bottled Water you should have no trouble at all keeping busy!

When prospective clients call or email you, explain about your Bottled Water, any special services you provide and your prices. With your customised service it is best to either ask for a 50% deposit or a 100% payment. This is because once you have delivered, it is sometimes hard to obtain the payment due. Make sure that you receive all the payment due before you finish the service.

First Contact

When a prospective customer calls, have your appointment book and a pen handy. Be friendly and enthusiastic. Explain what you do and offer to show a few samples.

Profitable New Bottled Water Business

When they ask how much you charge, simply give them a wide range and say that you will give a firm cost quote, once you've discussed their requirements. Then without much of a pause, ask if 4:30 this afternoon would be convenient for them, or if 5:30 would be better.

You must pointedly ask if they can meet at a certain time, or the decision may be put off, and you may come up with a "no sale." You may prefer to visit them if you do not have a suitable reception area.

Just as soon as you have an agreement on the time and place to make you proposal and marked it in your appointment book, ask for their name, address and telephone number.

Jot this information down on a 3 by 5 card, along with the date and the notation: Prospective Customer. Then you file this card in a permanent card file. Save these cards, because there are literally hundreds of ways to turn this prospect file into real cash, once you've accumulated a sizeable number of names, addresses and phone numbers. If you are comfortable with a computer, you can enter them straight into your CRM system. (Customer Management)

The Meeting

When you go to see your prospect in person, always be on time. A couple of minutes early won't hurt you, but a few minutes late will definitely be detrimental to your closing the sale. If they are coming to you then ensure that you give good directions and are ready for them.

Always be well groomed. Dress as a successful business owner. Be confident and sure of yourself; be knowledgeable about what you can do as well as understanding of the prospect's needs and wants. Do not smoke, even if invited by the prospect, and never accept a drink - even coffee - until after you have a signed contract in your briefcase. It's important to appear methodical, thorough and professional

A little small talk after the sale is appropriate, but becoming too friendly is not. You create an impression, and preserve it, by maintaining a business-like relation ship.

When you go to your meeting, take along a notebook, a calculator, your appointment book, some samples and your sales pack.

You should have at least two of your sales packs (one for the customer and the rest for her friends that may also need your services) and a blank contract (more of this later). A receipt book would also be a good idea. You can buy folios in stationary stores that will keep these all tidy.

If they choose one of standard Bottled Waters, fine, but if they want a particular design of their own, now is the time to ask for photos or start jotting down all their requirements, including sizes and colours.

You should hopefully come up with a drawing of what they require in front of them. Get them to sign off these details and picture so that there is no dispute later. You will probably have to come back to them with a firm price. Make sure that it is possible for you to actually produce this label for your Bottled Water as well as the bottle size!

Discuss when they need the Bottled Water and if you are delivering the Bottled Water or if they are collecting it from you.

Now complete the contract for them, summarizing what you have just agreed and confirm that you will send her a formal confirmation of your agreement. Ask them for confirmation on the contract and for a deposit if applicable. Also offer them a sales pack for their friend who may need your services.

The Art of Selling

It has been said that a sale is really closed long before the seller makes the final pitch to the customer. In many ways, this is very true. Many customers make a decision to buy in five minutes or less of being introduced to the product. As a successful entrepreneur, it is up to you to make those five minutes really count.

There are a couple of important things that take place in this five minute window of opportunity.

First, the customer decides whether or not it is worth the time to learn more about the product. If the answer is no, then even thirty minutes of a great pitch will accomplish nothing.

Second, the customer will think of major obstacles that will prevent the purchase from taking place. If a customer decides the product is out of reach for some reason, that will make everything that follows that first five minutes of no value whatsoever.

Your job is to overcome both these issues and encourage the prospect to not only desire the product, but also be able to visualise actively using the product to great advantage. Here are a few ideas on how to accomplish this:

- **Ascertain the needs of your client.** This means asking clarifying questions that help to narrow the focus of the presentation to what is important to the customer. For example, if a primary need of the client is to pay the phone bill at the end of the month, tailor the presentation to show how the product can directly help achieve that goal.

- **Be prepared to address common obstacles.** Many obstacles are not unique – people from all sorts of background will share the same concerns. Proactively bring those up during those first five minutes and quickly demonstrate how they are non-issues. This will make it possible to dispose of those concerns and hold the attention and interest of the prospect past that five minute window.

- **Always close with benefits**. Some of those benefits may have to do with overcoming obstacles, but go a little further than that. Using the phone bill example again, point out how the product can make it easier every month to pay the bill – not just the one that is due the end of this month.

Making the most of those first five minutes will greatly increase your chances of closing the sale. Spend some time working on a model presentation and critique the results. This will help you move with greater prowess when the real deal comes along.

Congratulations you have just made a sale!

Administration

Administration is very important. Without good administration your company will quickly disintegrate into chaos and you won't know who has what and who needs to pay for services and who needs them to be cleaned and when. Your administration should include ways of controlling or managing the following:

- Collecting money from your customers
- Banking money.
- Managing enquiries and complaints.
- Invoice and bill payment.
- Accounts and book keeping including, payroll, banking, taxes and VAT/taxes.
- Purchasing and auditing equipment. At least once a year and preferably quarterly, equipment must be checked against your accounts and for the need to be repaired.
- Salary and commission payments.
- Staff training and development.

It may seem a lot, but if you start small and get yourself a good accounts package, a good accountant and bank manager it is a lot easier.

Customer Administration

It is far better to use a CRM (Customer Management) software programme. These can be bought quite cheaply and are easy to understand. They will allow you to manage your customers and save customer data for marketing later on.

- Set up a file for each of your customers with their contact details, what you have agreed to do, the price to be charged and any other details. Keep a folder/file for each customer. Add each order to the file – latest order on top.

- The file should include all contact details. If you have a number of orders per client put a list of orders on top and tick them off as you complete them

- If you have a lot of customers have a customer number format.

- You should also keep a record of money due and paid. You should be able to find a good accounting system very easily. Always give a receipt.

- Make a To-Do list of all your orders and tick off those that have been completed. Put in order of importance/when delivered.

- Keep a detailed diary of when they have to be delivered by. In the diary also note what extra services were requested and what payment you need for the service.

Keep a diary of what money is due when and by who – refer to it each day and chase that money! Keep invoices separate to use for your accounts and to keep track of what you are owed.

Putting Your Business On The Internet

Just about anyone can put a web site up on the internet and now days it is quite easy. You have two choices as how to set up your website:

- As a shop window for your company, with contact details etc.
- As a fully working site with ecommerce facilities.

Which ever option you choose, you first need a god domain name. Go to a good domain provider like enom, Godaddy, namecheap NOT registerfly and spend under £10 on a domain. Choose a domain name that has the word dating, love etc in it. This will help with your search engine positioning as well as act as a memory jog to your potential customers.

As A Shop Window

Hop over to hostgator or similar and then buy a monthly hosting account. With that will come a site maker - where you can easily set up a web site using one of thousands of templates. You can add payment processor linkages, forums etc.

The only problem you will have is you want to sell promote or talk about illegal activities, terrorist activities or sex or have a high usage activity such as Myspace etc.

As A Full Site

You will probably need to get this especially written and designed for you. Put your project on sites like guru/elance/scriptlance etc and find a competitive quote.

Get yourself a PayPal account or similar so that you can take payment on your web site. This is much more secure and quicker than taking checks.

Factors To Remember

Always consider your target market when designing your web site. Include some helpful information about your subject matter but nothing that will give away what you are trying to sell!

Ensure that your contact details can be freely found and that details of your company and services are clearly set out.

As you will be asking for money before you deliver something – make your potential customer feel comfortable making payment and tell them what will happen next.

Respond to all enquiries and purchases very quickly. If this is difficult then set up an autoresponder to confirm you have received their enquiry/payment and will get back to them within a few hours.

Place references that you have received from past customers to show that you are a professional company.

Your challenge will be to be listed in the major search engines and then get traffic. Now market your web site like mad. It will take several months to make an impact in the major search engines. So build up your local custom whilst you are doing this. www.GetIntoGoogleFast.com – Does exactly what is says in the domain!

An Internet Marketing Strategy

O k, you've got your web site set up, you are sure that it is search engine friendly and you are pretty certain what your customers want. You've identified at least 3 products that you want to promote and you think that they meet your potential customer's needs. So now what?

Well unfortunately the days, that I can remember, of "build it and they will come" have long gone. Unless you promote your web site – no one will know that you are there and no visitors means no sales. So where so you go from here? Well take a deep breath, a pen and paper and let's start on your Marketing Strategy.

Briefly for a new business, with a relatively inexperienced marketer, your strategy will probably include the following options:

- Pay Per Click Advertising
- Article Marketing
- Email Marketing
- Community Marketing
- Classified Advertising

So let's get started – and before you start panicking, you are just writing your Marketing Strategy. This chapter will explain how to do all of the following.

Internet Advertising Kit

For each of your programs/products

- Write a short advert – say 50 words.
- Write a very short advert – say 15 words
- Write a short article – say about 400 – 600 words.
- Decide on your keywords – say about 30 – 50 words.

Internet Marketing Kit

For your web site theme

- Write at least 6 short auto responder messages.
- Find or write at least 2 giveaway products.

Internet Marketing Tools

- Your web site
- An autoresponder
- A good email account

Internet Marketing Strategy

Now let's put all of these together into your first Marketing Strategy.

- **Submit your web site to all the major search engines.** This will start to get your web site noticed. As this takes a long time, it needs to be the first thing that you do. You can do this yourself or pay someone else to do this for you. We provide this service for our customers for £20 a month, which includes submission to Google, Yahoo and MSN.

- **Set up your autoresponder form** on your web site and load your messages into the autoresponder. Ensure that you offer one of the giveaway products as a bonus for signing onto your ezine. The second giveaway can be set up for message 3 or 4. Your messages should be sent in the following intervals. Day 1,3,7,7,7,7

- **Set up your download pages**, for your bonus products as well as the products you are selling. Ensure that you provide an extra offer on each download page.

- **Submit your article** – including your resource box, to about 6 major ezine article sites. Limit yourself to 6 at the moment. Each of these submissions, if accepted will give you a link to your web site. If too many links to your new web site appear very quickly, search engines assume that you have been using "black hat" SEO tactics (a total no no) and will not list your site.

- **Identify 4 forums** that discuss the topics of your web site. Set yourself up an account name that describes you well. We use the name "Biz Guru" which is our trade mark and name. Set up your signature to include your web site address. You now have 4 good links to your web site.

- **Answer Questions:** Start answering questions asked within the forums. Do NOT post adverts for your web site or products. Use this time to establish your credentials. If you answer questions well and contribute to the forums, your web site tag will be noticed.

- **Set up a PPC campaign** – you can start with the smaller search engines first. Take your very small advert and your keywords and use them in your campaign. Most search engines will help you with your choice of keywords. Remember to set a budget and test, test and test again until you get quality and converting traffic.

- **Set up some classified ads**. You can do this one of two ways: i) choose one or two major sites/email lists and advertise with them. ii) use an ezine ad blaster to send your ad out to numerous lower quality places.

- **Test, Update and Modify**. Review, change and add to your PPC keywords. Submit more articles and adverts. Start tactfully promoting your products in the forums.

Well that's what to do to be a success. Good Luck.

Expanding

Expansion means growth, involving people working for you, more jobs to sell, and greater profits. Don't let it frighten you, for you have gained experience by starting gradually. After all - your aim in starting a business of your own was to make money, wasn't it? And expanding means more helpers so you don't have to work your self to death!

Staff

So, just as soon as you possibly can, recruit and hire other people to do the work for you. The first people you hire should be people to handle the basic work that you do..

You can obtain good staff by word of mouth, advertising in your local Job Centre, supermarket etc. Look in your local university and local school and ask amongst friends.

You will find a lot of people who want to work part time here which you will need at the start of your business.

You can start these people at minimum wage or a bit above, and train them to complete every job assignment in two hours or less. You might consider hiring people on a contract basis so that if they don't work you don't pay. You don't get loyalty here though.

You should also outfit them in a kind of uniform with your company name on the back of their blouses or shirts. A good idea would be to have magnetic signs made for your company and services. Place these signs on the sides of the cars your people use for transportation to each job, and later on, the sides of your company van or pick-up trucks.

Advertising

A good supply of business cards wouldn't be a bad idea for them either, in order to advertise your services to others they come in contact with. The only other form of advertising you should go with would be a display ad in the yellow pages of your telephone directory.

Customer Contracts

When you're dealing with customers, sometimes things can go wrong. It might be your fault, it might be their fault or it might be no-one's fault -- but if you didn't make a contract, then you'll all suffer.

Why Do I Need Contracts?

A contract gives you a sound legal base for your business, and some guarantee that you're going to get paid for your work without you having to ask the customer for payment in advance. In the event of a dispute, the contract lays down what the agreement was so that you can point to it and say what was agreed. If you ever end up having to go to court (let's hope you won't), the contract is what the judge's decision will be based on.

Without a contract, you leave yourself vulnerable and open to exploitation. Someone could claim that the terms they agreed with you were different to what you say they were or that they never signed up for anything at all and so they won't pay.

It's especially common to see big businesses mistreat small ones, thinking that they won't have the knowledge or the money to do anything about it. Essentially, contracts take away your customers' ability to hold non-payment over your head, and give you the ability to hold it over theirs instead.

Written and Verbal Contracts

It is important to point out the distinction in the law between a verbal (spoken) contract and a proper, written one. A verbal contract is binding in theory, but in practice can be very hard to prove. A written contract, on the other hand, is rock-solid proof of what you're saying.

You might think that you're never going to get into a dispute with your customers, but it's all too common to find yourself in a little disagreement.

They will often want to get you to do some 'small' amount of extra work to finish the job or make it better; not realizing that doing so would completely obliterate your profit margin.

For this reason, you should be very wary of doing anything with nothing but a verbal contract. On the other hand, if you were incautious or too trusting and only got a verbal contract, it could still go some way towards helping you, especially if there were witnesses.

Won't It Be Expensive?

Written contracts don't necessarily need to be formal contracts, which are drawn up by a lawyer with 'contract' written at the top and signed by both parties.

These kinds of contracts are the most effective, but can be expensive to have produced, not to mention intimidating to customers.

The most common kind of written contract, oddly enough, is a simple letter. If you send a customer a letter laying out your agreement before you start work, and they write back to agree to it, that is enough to qualify as a written contract, with most of the protections it affords. It is best to get confirmation from your customer that they have received this contract.

If you are doing high-value work for some clients, though, it could be worth the time and trouble of having your lawyer write a formal contract, or at least of doing it yourself and getting a lawyer to look it over.

Formal contracts will give you more protection if the worst happens, and there's nothing to stop you from making it a one-off expense only by re-using the same contract for multiple customers. PLEASE: TAKE PROFESSIOANAL ADVICE.

Contracts for Small Purchases.

Obviously it would be silly to expect everyone who buys some £10 product or service from you to sign a contract, or write back indicating their agreement to your terms. In this situation, you should have a statement of the 'terms and conditions' that your customer is agreeing to by buying from you, and they should have to tick some kind of box indicating their agreement before you send anything.

The Top 5 First-Year Mistakes

Even once you've got past the starting-up stage, there are still plenty mistakes to be made, and most of them are going to be made in your make-or-break year -- the first one. Here are the top five things to avoid.

Waiting for Customers to Come to You

Too many people wait for their customers to phone, or come to the door, or whatever. They get one or two customers through luck, but nothing like enough to even begin paying their costs. These people sit around, looking at their competitors doing lots of business, and wonder what they're doing wrong.

You can't be like this. You have to go out there and actively try to find customers. Talk to people, call them, meet with them -- whatever you do, don't just sit there!

Spending Too Much on Advertising

So everyone tells you that the only way to get ahead in business is to advertise. Well, that's true, but you need to make sure that you stick to inexpensive advertising methods when you're starting out. Spending hundreds of pounds for an ad in the local newspaper might turn out to get you very few new customers, and you will have spent your entire advertising budget on it.

Make your money go further with leaflets, direct mail or email -- these are easily targetable campaign methods with high response rates and low costs. Remember that it is always better to spend money on an offer than on an ad, and always better to spend money on an ad than on a delivery method.

Being Too Nice

When you're running your own business, it can be tempting to be everyone's friend, giving discounts at the drop of a hat and making sure that you don't hassle or inconvenience anyone.

That's all well and good, until you find that your Good Samaritan act has just halved your profit margin without lowering the cost to the customer by very much at all.

Sometimes, you need to realize that you've got to be harsh to make a profit. Give people discounts to encourage them to buy or to come back, not because you like them or feel sorry for them. Don't be afraid to be ruthless in your pursuit of business success. Nice guys don't finish last, but they are running in a different race -- one with much less prize money. If that doesn't bother you, of course, then feel free to go for it.

Not Using the Phone

You'd be surprised just how common phone fears are -- if you're scared of the phone, you're not alone by any means. Many people are terrified of making phone calls, and avoid them wherever possible. I have seen more than one business owner reduced to tears on the phone and trying desperately to hide it from the customer.

Profitable New Bottled Water Business

You need to try your best to overcome your fears, as talking to customers on the phone is almost as good as meeting them for real. Letters and emails are useless by comparison. The best way to overcome phone fears varies from person to person, but it can often be as simple as making the phone fun, by calling friends and relatives often for a while and getting used to it. Alternatively, try working in telemarketing for a while -- if that doesn't make normal phone use look like a walk in the park by comparison, then nothing will.

Hiring Professionals for Everything

It can be tempting to think that, since you're starting out, you should just find a company or person to do every little thing you need. People seem to especially overspend on design services.

You might think it'd be great to have fancy graphics all over your website, but would it really increase sales? If I saw it, it would put me right off. Likewise, a slick brochure often fails to say anything more than 'I'm going to charge you a premium to pay for my expensive brochures'.

Don't hire someone unless you can demonstrate that the service they're going to provide will increase your profits by more than the amount you're spending -- if you're not sure, try it yourself first, and you can always upgrade it later.

Problems You May Have

As in any business you will get problems, sometimes just knowing what you may face is a great help.

- Some customers use office email to correspond with you. Make sure that you are discrete with the headings used on the emails to them.

- Some customers are never satisfied. Just make any reasonable changes that are requested. Be polite and patient.

- Some customers may have problems explaining what they want – this is where your product sheet comes in handy. Make sure that you write down everything that they request and get this agreed to.

- Some customers are very slow in replying – ensure that you give them a time limit to reply and then send two further reminders – telling them when the last one is.

Time for a Holiday: But How?

When you've been working long and hard at your business for a while, you might feel like you've earned yourself a little break. There are business owners out there who haven't taken a real holiday since they started their business -- including some who started their business as long as five years ago!

After all, how can you ever just desert your business and your customers and go bronze yourself on the beach? How can you avoid being on call 24/7 throughout your holiday? Well, everyone deserves some time to themselves at least once a year, if they want to keep being productive and avoid stress. Here's what to do.

Tell People When You Are Going Away.

You can't just disappear when you're running a business -- you need to let people know long in advance that you're not going to be available, and make sure that they have everything they need to manage without you while you're away. It's best to schedule your holiday not to interfere too much with the business.

However much you might want to have your holiday in the summer, it's important to remember that every business has its quiet months, and you should schedule your holiday in the period where they seem to be.

Change Your Voicemail Message.

A quick and simple way to let people know that you've gone away is to change your voicemail message.

This allows you to still hear what people have to say when you get back, and stops them from wondering why you never seem to answer your phone.

A good format for the message is as follows: 'Hi, this is [your name] at [company name]. I'm sorry I'm not in the office right now, but I will be back on [give a date]. If you leave a message, I will be sure to get back to you'.

If you work from home don't give a coming back date unless you want to invite the local thief into your home!

Set Up an Email Auto responder.

Similar to a voicemail message, but less commonly used, is the email auto responder. Again, you don't want people to wonder why their emails are going unanswered, so your best bet is to set up your email program to automatically reply to any email you get with a message saying that you've gone away.

Example: 'Hello, and thank you for your email. This is an auto responder, as I'm away on holiday until [date]. I have received your email, however, and will respond to it upon my return. I apologies for any inconvenience to you, and I am willing to make an offer of 10% off your next order to make it up to you.' The special offer for people who get the auto responder is a nice touch -- it makes them feel lucky that they emailed you while you were away, instead of frustrated.

Don't Stay Away Too Long.

Of course, when you go on holiday, you're relying on people being willing to wait for you. That means you can't really take the kids to Disney World for two weeks, or spend a month staying with a friend abroad -- it's just too long to be away from your business for.

You should regard a weekend away as ideal (it avoids the whole problem for the most part), and a week as the maximum you can allow yourself. Don't let people make you feel bad about only taking one-week holidays: after all, you could always have more than one each year.

Alternatively: Get Someone to Look after the Business.

If you really want to get away for longer, or it's essential that your customers don't have any break in service, then you could consider getting someone to look after your business. This could be an existing member of staff that you make your 'deputy', to be in charge while you're away, or it could be someone who's related to you and has some experience running a business. You could even hand the business over to a competitor that you're friendly with and share the profits with them, if you think they're trustworthy and they could handle it. Enjoy your holiday!

In Conclusion

One of the most important aspects of this business is asking for, and allowing your customers to refer other prospects to you. All of this happens, of course, as a result of your giving fast, dependable service. You might even set up a promotional notice on the back of your business card (to be left as each job is completed) offering £5 off their next bill when they refer you to a new prospect.

This is definitely a high profit business, requiring an investment of time and organisation on your part to get started. With a low investment, little or no over head requirement, and no experience needed, this is an ideal business opportunity with a growth curve that accelerates at an unprecedented rate. Think about it. If it appeals to you, set up your own plan of operations and go for it! The profit potential for an owner of this type of business is outstanding! Good Luck.

Index

Profitable New Bottled Water Business

www.ingramcontent.com/pod-product-compliance
Lightning Source LLC
Chambersburg PA
CBHW031813190326
41518CB00006B/313